D0776825

How to Wok
up a
Storm Without
Burning
the House
Down

Easy
Asian
Recipes

This book has no connection with
a well-known film star,
living or not living in a jungle,
who has or may not have a tall wife

LAGOON
BOOKS

PUBLISHED IN 2001 BY
LAGOON BOOKS
PO BOX 311, KT2 5QW, UK
PO BOX 990676, BOSTON, MA 02199, USA
WWW.LAGOONGAMES.COM

ISBN: 1902813421

FIRST PUBLISHED IN AUSTRALIA IN 1998 BY
PAN MACMILLAN AUSTRALIA PTY LIMITED

COPYRIGHT © 1998 BILLY BLUE MERCHANDISING PTY LTD

RECIPES BY HELEN TRACEY AND LINDA KAPLAN

ADDITIONAL WRITING BY ROSS RENWICK

SUPERVISING CHEFS MATT BLUNDELL AND GAVIN CUMMINS
OF KENTRA DOUBLE BAY AUSTRALIA

MANAGING DIRECTOR AARON KAPLAN   CREATIVE DIRECTOR ROSS RENWICK

PRINTED IN SINGAPORE

NOT TOM CRUISE

A FEW YEARS AGO I'M FLYING A MIG 36 ALL-WEATHER FIGHTER JUST NORTH OF HO CHI MINH CITY. I'VE STOLEN IT FROM A RUSSIAN AIR FORCE BASE WHICH IS MY OTHER JOB. I'M DELIVERING IT TO AN ARMS DEALER WHOSE NAME I AM TOO PRUDENT TO MENTION HERE.

I SENSE A PRESENCE AND LOOK UP. AND THERE, UPSIDE DOWN AND RIGHT ABOVE ME, IS TOM BLOODY CRUISE IN A US NAVY TOM CAT FIGHTER-BOMBER, GIVING ME THE FINGER. HE'S ACTING PRETTY AGGRESSIVE AND HOW AM I TO KNOW THAT HE'S MAKING A MOVIE CALLED TOP GUN? SO I SHOOT HIM DOWN.

ANYWAY, BECAUSE OF THE EXTRA REVVING, I RUN OUT OF PETROL OR KEROSENE OR WHATEVER THESE THINGS USE AND PARACHUTE TO THE GROUND. HERE I MEET A VERY NICE VIETNAMESE MAN CALLED TRANG DO. TOM CRUISE IS WITH HIM AND NOT MAKING MUCH SENSE BECAUSE OF A KNOCK TO THE HEAD.

A FEW MINUTES LATER A HELICOPTER ARRIVES WITH THE DIRECTOR OF THE FILM. HE SEES THAT TOM ISN'T MAKING MUCH SENSE. HE LOOKS AT HIS HELICOPTER PILOT WHO LOOKS A BIT LIKE TOM. HE ASKS TRANG DO IF THERE'S ANY PLASTIC SURGEONS AROUND HERE. THERE IS. CLINT, THE HELICOPTER PILOT, IS ALTERED TO LOOK LIKE TOM. GOD, THIS STORY IS COMPLICATED.

AFTER A FEW DAYS THEY LEAVE TO SHOOT THE REST OF THE FILM. BUT WITHOUT TOM. TOM IS HAVING A NICE TIME TALKING TO THE MOON AND SMILING, AND LOVING VIETNAMESE FOOD. AS YOU KNOW, HE'S GOT A GREAT SMILE AND THE LOCALS

REALLY LIKE HIM.

I STAY IN THE JUNGLE FOR TWO YEARS BECAUSE
TRANG DO IS THE MOST FAMOUS CHEF IN
VIETNAM.
I LEARN HIS SECRET RECIPES, THE ONES IN THIS
BOOK, PASSED DOWN FOR CENTURIES. TOM AND I
COOK NEW RECIPES EVERY DAY. TOM HAS BECOME
ONE OF THE MOST FAMOUS CHEFS IN VIETNAM.
TOM STAYS. I LEAVE.

HAVE A LOOK AT THE VIDEO OF TOP GUN.
NOTICE THERE ARE TWO SLIGHTLY DIFFERENT
TOM CRUISES. THE NEW ONE IS JUST A BIT
SHORTER.

BUT KEEP IT TO YOURSELF, BECAUSE I DON'T
THINK NICOLE KNOWS.

ACTUAL
PHOTOGRAPH
OF INCIDENT

CLAUDIA SOUP

I don't want to be boastful about this, but I was cycling through Vietnam with a supermodel whose identity shall not be mentioned here as I am a man of honour, but she is a tall blonde and her first name is Claudia.

The cycling had been easy, more or less, as the country around the Mekong Delta is flat, but Kevin Bacon is very poor on a bicycle and we had to constantly wait for him.

Looking back, we could see him several kilometres behind struggling up the only hill in the area, so we diverted down a narrow pathway towards a monastery that we could see glowing whitely on a distant hill.

I suppose it had passed through both our minds that Kevin could miss us altogether and we would not have to put up with him talking about his blisters, at least until tomorrow.

But an hour later we were bogged in a narrower pathway. Claudia was getting bad tempered and I was tired when we came by a small grass hut.

An ancient woman came towards us, smiling.

'I have been waiting for you, my son,' she said. 'A wise man not in the company of Kevin Bacon but yet a man who knows the secret of Elvis Michalopolous. A man in the company of a famous blonde woman whose name must not be mentioned.'

She went to the hut and came back with a piece of paper, folded many times, ancient and stained.

I did not like stained.

'I was told that you would come,' she said. 'And that you would read this.'

I opened the paper. On the front was a map showing us the way to the monastery. On the other side was faint writing. It was a recipe for Mien Xao Thit Ga, which because of the oath that I took at the monastery, can only be known as Claudia with No Second Name Chicken with Green Beans and Noodles.

MIEN XAO THIT GA

CHICKEN WITH GREEN BEANS AND NOODLES

SERVES 4.

- **150g/5oz BEAN THREAD VERMICELLI NOODLES**
- **1 TABLESPOON PEANUT OIL**
- **500g/1lb CHICKEN THIGH FILLETS, HALVED**
- **250g/9oz GREEN BEANS**
- **2 CLOVES GARLIC, CRUSHED**
- **1 MEDIUM ONION, FINELY SLICED**
- **2 TABLESPOONS FISH SAUCE**
- **2 TABLESPOONS SOY SAUCE**
- **2 TEASPOONS LIME JUICE**

1 TABLESPOON CORNFLOUR

1 TABLESPOON WATER

2 TABLESPOONS CHOPPED FRESH BASIL

2 TABLESPOONS CHOPPED MINT

SOAK VERMICELLI NOODLES IN WARM WATER UNTIL SOFT, DRAIN.

SEAL CHICKEN IN WOK WITH HALF THE PEANUT OIL.

DRAIN ON ABSORBENT PAPER.

BOIL, STEAM OR MICROWAVE BEANS UNTIL JUST TENDER.

RINSE UNDER COLD WATER, DRAIN.

ADD REMAINING OIL TO WOK, FRY ONION AND GARLIC BRIEFLY THEN ADD NOODLES, BEANS, SAUCES, JUICE AND BLENDED CORNFLOUR AND WATER.

STIR OVER HEAT UNTIL MIXTURE BOILS AND THICKENS.

STIR IN BASIL AND MINT.

A frustrated investor in the south of Vietnam once said something along the lines of…'What can you expect from a people that have had a thousand years of Mandarin rule, a hundred years of the French civil service (which makes Yes Minister look like an efficiency manual), then a couple of decades of being saved by the Americans and then communism.'

After all that time and trouble it is the French that seemed to have had the greatest influence. On one side of the road there's McDonald's. On the other there's a French cafe. I know where I'm heading.

There is a European theory that regular invasions of France by Germany have had little to do with politics or land, but much to do with food. As far as anyone knows, Germany has never been invaded by a country seeking their food.

MIEN XAO TOM

CORIANDER GARLIC PRAWNS AND NOODLES

SERVES 6.

1kg/2 lb THICK FRESH RICE NOODLES

1 TABLESPOON PEANUT OIL

1 MEDIUM ONION, SLICED

1 1/2 CLOVES GARLIC, FINELY CHOPPED

750g/1 3/4 lb MEDIUM UNCOOKED PRAWNS, SHELLED, DEVEINED, HALVED

3 GREEN SHALLOTS, CHOPPED

- **100g/2 CUPS BEAN SPROUTS**
- **4 TABLESPOONS FRESH CORIANDER LEAVES**
- **2 MEDIUM TOMATOES, PEELED, SEEDED, CHOPPED**
- **2 TABLESPOONS FINELY CHOPPED UNSALTED ROASTED PEANUTS**

PLACE NOODLES IN BOWL, COVER WITH WARM WATER, STAND FOR 5 MINUTES, THEN DRAIN.

HEAT OIL IN PAN, ADD ONION AND GARLIC AND COOK, STIRRING UNTIL ONION IS GOLDEN.

ADD PRAWNS, STIRRING FOR A FEW MINUTES OR UNTIL PRAWNS ARE PINK AND TENDER.

STIR IN SHALLOTS AND SPROUTS, COOL FOR 10 MINUTES.

TOP NOODLES WITH PRAWN MIXTURE, CORIANDER, TOMATOES AND PEANUTS, DRIZZLE WITH DRESSING.

SERVE WARM OR COLD.

DRESSING:

- **60ml/1/4 CUP LIME JUICE**
- **60ml/1/4 CUP FISH SAUCE**
- **1 SMALL FRESH RED CHILLI, SEEDED, FINELY CHOPPED**
- **1 1/2 CLOVES GARLIC, FINELY CHOPPED**
- **1 TEASPOON SUGAR**
- **COMBINE ALL INGREDIENTS IN A BOWL, MIX WELL**

ROBERT DE NIRO FISH

We'd gone down to Halong Bay from Hanoi. Nelson Mandela said to me, 'Ziggy, it's your birthday, you choose your crew.'

I chose Janis Joplin, Elvis Presley, Tom Cruise, and of course, me.

We had two Hawaiian-style racing canoes, four-oarers, and we were going to race from the Hong Gai ferry to Cat Hai Island. About 20 kilometres.

After I chose Joplin, Presley, Cruise and Zen the other crew ended up as Nelson Mandela, Bill Clinton, Boris Yeltsin and for the girls, Doris Day.

We were about a century younger than the Mandela, Clinton, Yeltsin, Day crew so we allowed that they could also have Kevin Bacon, who no-one had wanted.

We left Hong Gai and began paddling south-west across the widest part of the bay. Several kilometres into the bay, the Bai Chai ferry, a nasty rusting hulk, passed us on the starboard side and created a very large bow wave.

We paddled the canoes close together and pointed their bows towards the wave.

The wave hit us both at the same time and the bows rose high in the air before they slapped safely into the water.

Nelson said, 'Well done, brave sailors.'

Kevin Bacon stood up and shouted, 'What... (unfinished sentence)', and fell into our boat which sank. The Mandela, Clinton, Yeltsin, Day crew moved their boat towards us, struggling in the water, and in a flash Kevin Bacon grabbed the side of their boat and tried to hoist himself into it. Turned it upside down, he did.

To cut a long story short, we couldn't right the second boat, so we clung to it.

Night fell and we chatted among ourselves to keep our spirits up.

At what we thought was about midnight, Kevin said...'I have a story to tell you.

'This afternoon I met an old Vietnamese chef called Cat Ba who said he had been guarding a secret recipe for fifty years...a recipe that could never be spoken, but only written down, or it would disappear from history. The Japanese, the French and the Americans all tried to get the recipe from Cat Ba but never succeeded. This afternoon Cat Ba died in my arms, but before he did, he wrote this recipe in the sand and I memorised it.

'I am weakening,' continued Kevin Bacon, 'so with my Swiss army knife I am going to scratch the recipe in the side of this boat. If any of you survive then you are the keepers of the recipe.'

Kevin then drifted away, repeatedly calling a mournful cry that sounded like...'I thought I was very good in that film with Robert de Niro...'

We never saw Kevin again.

ROBERT DE NIRO FISH
ALSO KNOWN AS **CA KHO NUOC DUA**

BRAISED FISH IN COCONUT JUICE
SERVES 4.

ABOUT 1kg/2 lb, OR ABOUT 4 FILLETS, OF BLUE EYE COD, BREAM OR SNAPPER

4 TABLESPOONS FISH SAUCE

$1/4$ TEASPOON SALT

1 TABLESPOON SUGAR, IF USING COCONUT JUICE

1 TEASPOON CARAMEL SAUCE

JUICE OF ONE COCONUT, OR 1 400ml CAN/$3/4$ PINT COCONUT MILK

500ml/2 CUPS WATER

CUT FISH FILLETS INTO 4 cm PIECES.

MARINATE FILLETS IN FISH SAUCE, SALT, SUGAR (IF USING COCONUT JUICE) AND CARAMEL SAUCE FOR ONE HOUR.

BOIL COCONUT JUICE (OR MILK) AND WATER IN A SAUCEPAN OVER MODERATE HEAT.

ADD FISH AND MARINADE TO COCONUT MIXTURE, MAKING SURE THERE IS ENOUGH LIQUID TO COVER FISH.

BOIL FOR FIVE MINUTES, SKIMMING OFF FOAM.

REDUCE HEAT AND SIMMER FOR 30 MINUTES.

1 whole Bream
Fish sauce
salt
Sugar
Caramel sauce
coconut milk

"I THOUGHT I WAS VERY GOOD IN THAT FILM WITH ROBERT DE NIRO"

NOODLES

BUY FROM ASIAN FOOD STORES AND SUPERMARKETS.

MIEN – CELLOPHANE OR BEAN THREAD.

MADE FROM MUNG BEANS AND PEAS.

BUN – RICE VERMICELLI.

COOKED AND SERVED COLD IN SALADS.
ADD TO SOUPS.

BANH PHO – FRESH RICE, LOOKS LIKE FETTUCCINE.

BASIS OF PHO SOUPS.

HU TIEU – RICE STICKS MADE FROM RICE FLOUR.
COME IN VARIOUS STYLES.

USED IN SOUPS AND STIR-FRIES.

WHAT TO SERVE UP AS WELL

IN SMALL BEAUTIFUL BOWLS, TAKE YOUR PICK.

FISH SAUCE

LIME WEDGES

SLICED CHILLIES

CHILLI SAUCE

DIPPING SAUCES (SEE RECIPES, OR ADD YOUR OWN INGREDIENTS TO FISH SAUCE — SAY TAMARIND OR GINGER)

PICKLES

SALADS

CHOPPED HERBS

BEAN SPROUTS

SWEET CHILLI SAUCE

SOY SAUCE

CLASSIC DIPPING SAUCE

I'm not going to make a big thing out of this. But in a thousand years when Millennium 3 anthropologists are digging up my city they're going to find some pretty crappy bowls.

I live on the green edge of one of the planet's biggest deserts.

From my house I can see one of the world's biggest seas.

Parts of the year the wind from the desert can cook your eggs.

So when the anthropologists begin to dig up this city they'll think that drought will have buried this civilisation.

But they'll be wrong.

Pottery will have buried this civilisation.

Every vacant room and hall in this huge city has a pottery class happening in it. While the Millennium 3 anthropologists are digging through the 2 kilometres of pottery that has buried this city, the lead anthro will call them all together and say, 'It's early days yet but this city has created history. It is the world's most prolific manufacturer of really crappy brown bowls.'

You're not going to cook a camel's head in a wok, are you? So don't serve Nuoc Mam Cham Nguyen Chat in one of those brown bowls that your aunt makes.

NUOC MAM CHAM NGUYEN CHAT

CLASSIC DIPPING SAUCE

2 TABLESPOONS LIME JUICE

1 FRESH RED CHILLI

2 CLOVES GARLIC

1 TEASPOON SUGAR

1 TABLESPOON RICE VINEGAR

3 TABLESPOONS WATER

3 TABLESPOONS FISH SAUCE

2 TEASPOONS CARROT, SHREDDED

2 TEASPOONS WHITE RADISH, SHREDDED

FINELY CHOP CHILLI AND GARLIC.

POUND THE CHILLI, SUGAR AND GARLIC TO A FINE PASTE IN A MORTAR.

SLOWLY STIR IN THE VINEGAR, WATER AND LIME JUICE AND ADD THE FISH SAUCE LAST.

POUR OVER CARROTS AND RADISH.

STORE IN JAR, REFRIGERATE.

SHAKE BEFORE USE.

CAN BE SERVED WITH ANY/EVERY MAIN COURSE.

NUOC MAM THAM

Elvis Michalopoulos, the flash Greek from another book, claims to be the first person to import Vietnamese fish sauce into Greece, a business that was once likened to selling horse's heads to vegetarians.

Elvis also says he is the other better-known Elvis, and claims that the CIA won't let him back into America because all the pretend Elvises are ex-CIA agents. (It's their retirement program.)

Elvis lives to the east of Ho Chi Minh City, next door to a man who saw Kevin Bacon drive past and later went to an art gallery where Al Pacino had been the week before. The same man thinks that he keeps seeing Tom Cruise at the Ho Chi Minh City vegetable markets. Talk about six degrees of separation.

Anyway, Elvis and the guy who keeps seeing Tom Cruise spent years refining this recipe for coconut and fish sauce.

NUOC MAM THAM

COCONUT AND FISH SAUCE

- **1 TABLESPOON LIME JUICE**
- **1 TEASPOON FRESH LEMON GRASS, MINCED**
- **3 TABLESPOONS FISH SAUCE**
- **3 TABLESPOONS BOILED WATER**
- **1 TABLESPOON SUGAR**
- **60ml/$\frac{1}{4}$ CUP COCONUT MILK**

MIX ALL INGREDIENTS TOGETHER.

SERVE WITH NOODLES, FISH, OR JUST PUT IT ON THE TABLE WITH OTHER DIPPING SAUCES.

ELVIS MICHALOPOULOS

NUOC MAM

SIMPLE DIPPING SAUCE

¹/₂ TEASPOON SUGAR

3 TABLESPOONS FISH SAUCE

1 TABLESPOON FRESH LIME JUICE

1 FRESH RED CHILLI, SEEDED, FINELY SLICED

IN A SMALL SERVING BOWL, DISSOLVE THE SUGAR IN A LITTLE OF THE FISH SAUCE.

ADD THE REST OF THE FISH SAUCE AND THE LIME JUICE AND CHILLI.

THIS SAUCE IS AVAILABLE AT EVERY MEAL IN VIETNAM, AND CAN BE EATEN WITH ALL DISHES.

VERY EASY TO MAKE.

!

NUOC MAM TOI
LEMON AND GARLIC FISH SAUCE

3 CLOVES GARLIC, CRUSHED
JUICE OF 1 LEMON
3 TABLESPOONS SUGAR
125ml/$^1/_2$ CUP FISH SAUCE
125ml/$^1/_2$ CUP COLD WATER
1 CHILLI, SEEDED, SLICED (OPTIONAL)

MIX ALL INGREDIENTS TOGETHER.

SERVE WITH OTHER DIPPING SAUCES. GUESTS CAN CHOOSE THE FLAVOUR THEY PREFER.

CARAMEL SAUCE

2 TABLESPOONS FISH SAUCE
100g/4oz SUGAR
6 TABLESPOONS WATER

MIX SUGAR WITH 4 TABLESPOONS WATER IN SAUCEPAN.

COOK OVER LOW HEAT UNTIL BROWN.

ALLOW TO COOL AND THEN WITH EXTREME CARE, ADD REMAINDER OF WATER AND FISH SAUCE AND STIR UNTIL DISSOLVED.

REMOVE FROM HEAT.

\# THIS SAUCE MAY BE ADDED TO COOKED DISHES FOR FLAVOUR, BUT IS NOT GENERALLY SERVED AT THE TABLE.

DO CHUA
VIETNAMESE PICKLES

SERVES 6.

250g/2 CUPS WHITE RADISHES
250g/2 CUPS CARROT
2 TEASPOONS SALT
5 TABLESPOONS SUGAR
250ml/1 CUP VINEGAR

PEEL CARROT AND RADISHES.

SLICE THEM THINLY INTO SMALL STRIPS (JULIENNE).

ADD SALT.

MIX WELL, ALLOW TO STAND FOR 5 MINUTES.

RINSE WELL.

MIX SUGAR WITH VINEGAR.

MARINATE RADISHES AND CARROT IN THE SUGAR
AND VINEGAR MIXTURE FOR 1 HOUR.

KEEP CARROT AND RADISHES WITH THE LIQUID IN
AN AIR-TIGHT JAR.

REFRIGERATE UNTIL USE.

SERVE WITH A SALAD, IN A SANDWICH, OR WITH
ANY MAIN COURSE.

CA-ROT CHUA
PICKLED CARROT

500g/16oz CARROTS
3 RED CHILLIES, SLICED
3 CLOVES GARLIC, SLICED
500ml/2 CUPS RICE VINEGAR
250ml/1 CUP WATER
PINCH OF SUGAR
PINCH OF SALT

SLICE CARROTS INTO THIN STRIPS (JULIENNE).

PUT CARROTS, CHILLI AND GARLIC INTO JAR.

BOIL VINEGAR, WATER, SALT AND SUGAR
FOR 5 MINUTES.

COOL, POUR OVER VEGETABLES.

SEAL JAR.

LEAVE FOR 48 HOURS.

LASTS FOR 2-3 WEEKS.

THE GUITAR OF ELVIS MICHALOPOULOS

COM CHIEN
POT-ROASTED RICE

400g/14oz MEDIUM-GRAIN RICE
2 TABLESPOONS PEANUT OIL
625ml/2 1/2 CUPS HOT WATER

WASH AND DRAIN RICE WELL TO REMOVE EXCESS STARCH.

HEAT OIL IN A HEAVY SAUCEPAN WITH A WELL-FITTING LID.

FRY RICE, STIRRING GENTLY WITH A METAL SPOON, FOR 10-15 MINUTES OR UNTIL RICE BECOMES OPAQUE AND TURNS GOLDEN BROWN.

ADD HOT WATER, BRING TO BOIL, THEN REDUCE TO VERY LOW HEAT.

STIR, THEN COVER AND COOK FOR 20 MINUTES.

SERVE WITH NUOC MAM CHAM NGUYEN CHAT (SEE PAGE 19) AND OTHER DISHES.

\# IF USING LONG-GRAIN RICE, INCREASE HOT WATER TO 500ml/2 1/2 CUPS FOR THE SAME RESULT.

BO GIO

VIETNAMESE BEEF SPRING ROLLS

RARE ROAST BEEF (THINLY SLICED) OR PRAWNS, CRABMEAT OR COOKED CHICKEN

CHOPPED CHILLI, BEAN SPROUTS, SHREDDED MINT, CORIANDER, BASIL LEAVES

GREEN PAPAYA, FINELY SLICED

A SQUIRT OF LEMON OR LIME JUICE

FISH SAUCE, SESAME OIL

LETTUCE

THIN RICE VERMICELLI/NOODLES (ABOUT 2 HANDFULS)

\# THE AMOUNT OF EACH INGREDIENT IS UP TO YOU, DEPENDING ON THE NUMBER OF PEOPLE WHO ARE EATING.

MINCE BEEF (OR ALTERNATIVE MEAT).

SOAK NOODLES IN A BOWL OF BOILING WATER UNTIL JUST SOFT, THEN DRAIN AND REFRESH WITH COLD WATER.

PAT DRY AND TOSS LIGHTLY WITH SESAME OIL.

MIX FILLING INGREDIENTS AND ADD NOODLES.

MIX WELL.

ADD LEMON OR LIME JUICE AND FISH SAUCE.

TO SERVE, PLACE SOME OF THE NOODLES AND BEEF MIXTURE IN A CRISP LETTUCE LEAF, ROLL UP AND EAT WITH YOUR FINGERS.

CANH XA-LACH-SON

PRAWN AND WATERCRESS SOUP

SERVES 6.

500g/1lb GREEN PRAWNS, SHELLED AND DEVEINED

2 SPRING ONIONS

2 TABLESPOONS VEGETABLE OIL

1 TEASPOON SUGAR

PINCH OF SALT

1 ½ LITRES/2 ½ PINTS WATER

2 TABLESPOONS FISH SAUCE

2 LARGE HANDFULS OF WATERCRESS

A DELICATE FLAVOUR, AND EASY TO MAKE.

FLATTEN THE PRAWNS WITH A PESTLE, CRUSHING THEM BUT LEAVING THEM INTACT.

CUT THE SPRING ONIONS INTO 2 ½ cm PIECES AND CRUSH LIGHTLY.

PUT THE OIL AND THE SPRING ONIONS INTO A SAUCEPAN AND HEAT UNTIL THE SPRING ONIONS HAVE WILTED.

ADD THE PRAWNS AND STIR OVER A MODERATE HEAT UNTIL THEY CHANGE COLOUR.

ADD THE SUGAR AND SALT TO THE SAUCEPAN, STIRRING FOR A FEW SECONDS, THEN POUR IN THE WATER.

STIR IN THE FISH SAUCE AND BRING TO THE BOIL.

ADD THE WATERCRESS.

SERVE IMMEDIATELY SO THAT THE WATERCRESS RETAINS ITS FRESH COLOUR.

VARIATION: WATERCRESS CAN BE REPLACED WITH BABY SPINACH LEAVES.

UNIMPORTANT MOP

CUA NAU CANH BOT BANG

ASPARAGUS AND CRAB SOUP

SERVES 4.

1250ml/5$\frac{1}{2}$ CUPS CHICKEN STOCK

2 TABLESPOONS FISH SAUCE

$\frac{1}{4}$ TEASPOON SALT

$\frac{1}{2}$ TEASPOON SUGAR

3 TEASPOONS VEGETABLE OIL

4 SHALLOTS, FINELY CHOPPED

2 CLOVES GARLIC, CHOPPED

200g/7oz CRABMEAT, FRESH OR CANNED

GROUND BLACK PEPPER

2 TABLESPOONS CORNFLOUR

2 TABLESPOONS WATER

2 EGGS, LIGHTLY BEATEN

200g/7oz FRESH ASPARAGUS

50g/$\frac{1}{2}$ CUP SHREDDED CORIANDER

COMBINE STOCK, 1 TABLESPOON FISH SAUCE, SUGAR AND SALT.

BRING TO BOIL, REDUCE AND SIMMER.

HEAT OIL, ADD SHALLOTS AND GARLIC, COOK UNTIL GOLDEN.

ADD CRABMEAT, 1 TABLESPOON FISH SAUCE AND BLACK PEPPER TO TASTE.

STIR AND FRY 1 MINUTE, SET ASIDE.

RETURN STOCK TO BOIL.

ADD CORNFLOUR MIXED WITH WATER.

STIR UNTIL SOUP THICKENS.

POUR EGG IN A THIN STREAM, STIRRING UNTIL
THREADS FORM.

ADD CRABMEAT AND ASPARAGUS, COOK UNTIL
ASPARAGUS IS TENDER.

ADD CORIANDER AND STIR.

SERVE.

THIS ELEPHANT WAS ONCE SEEN
IN THE COMPANY OF KEVIN BACON

SUP GA

CHICKEN AND CORN SOUP WITH
LEMON GRASS

SERVES 6.

**5 CHICKEN THIGH FILLETS (SKIN AND
FAT REMOVED)**

1 $1/2$ LITRES/$6 1/2$ CUPS WATER

**1 TABLESPOON CHOPPED FRESH
LEMON GRASS**

**1 TEASPOON FINELY CHOPPED
FRESH GINGER**

4 BLACK PEPPERCORNS

2 TEASPOONS PEANUT OIL

60g/2oz FRENCH SHALLOTS, CHOPPED

2 CLOVES GARLIC, CRUSHED

1 440g/16oz CAN CREAMED CORN

1 310g/11oz CAN CORN KERNELS

60ml/$1/4$ CUP FISH SAUCE

**3 TEASPOONS TAMARIND PULP
CONCENTRATE**

1 TABLESPOON CORNFLOUR

2 TABLESPOONS WATER, EXTRA

1 EGG, LIGHTLY BEATEN

**1 TABLESPOON CHOPPED FRESH
CORIANDER LEAVES**

1 TABLESPOON CHOPPED FRESH BASIL

COMBINE CHICKEN, WATER, LEMON GRASS, GINGER AND PEPPERCORNS IN LARGE PAN.

BRING TO BOIL AND SKIM.

SIMMER, UNCOVERED FOR 30 MINUTES, OR UNTIL CHICKEN IS TENDER.

STRAIN CHICKEN MIXTURE, RESERVE STOCK AND CHICKEN, AND DISCARD GINGER MIXTURE.

REMOVE CHICKEN FLESH FROM BONES, DISCARD BONES.

PULL CHICKEN FLESH INTO FINE SHREDS.

HEAT OIL IN CLEAN PAN, ADD SHALLOTS AND GARLIC, COOK, STIRRING, UNTIL SHALLOTS ARE SOFT, SET ASIDE.

STIR-FRY CHICKEN AND FISH SAUCE FOR 1 MINUTE, SET ASIDE, ADD EXTRA WATER, STIR OVER HEAT UNTIL MIXTURE BOILS AND THICKENS SLIGHTLY.

POUR EGG INTO SIMMERING SOUP UNTIL THREADS FORM, STIR IN HERBS. ADD RESERVED STOCK, CHICKEN, CREAMED CORN, CORN KERNELS, SAUCE AND TAMARIND.

ADD CORNFLOUR MIXTURE, STIR GENTLY UNTIL THICKENED.

\# A COMBINATION OF PUREED AND WHOLE-KERNEL CORN GIVES INTERESTING FLAVOUR AND TEXTURE TO THIS DELICIOUS SOUP.

PHO BO

BEEF SOUP WITH FRESH RICE NOODLES

SERVES 6-8.

THIS IS THE CLASSIC VIETNAMESE DISH, AVAILABLE EVERYWHERE IN VIETNAM, AND EATEN AT ALL TIMES OF DAY. IT CAN BE MADE WITH CHICKEN, BEEF OR PORK.

STOCK:

THIS IS BEST MADE THE DAY BEFORE.

- **1kg/2 lb BEEF SHIN BONES, SAWN INTO PIECES BY YOUR BUTCHER**
- **1 THUMB-SIZED KNOB OF FRESH GINGER, CHOPPED**
- **$1/2$ TEASPOON SALT**
- **3 LITRES/$5 1/4$ PINTS WATER**
- **500g/1lb BEEF BRISKET, CUT INTO PIECES**
- **1 CARROT, CHOPPED**
- **2 STALKS CELERY, CHOPPED**
- **4 TABLESPOONS FISH SAUCE (OR TO YOUR TASTE)**
- **2 CINNAMON STICKS**
- **2 STAR ANISE**
- **2 BROWN ONIONS, FINELY SLICED**

GRILL GINGER AND ONION UNTIL STICKS CHARRED, THEN PEEL OFF BURNT SKIN.

COMBINE ALL INGREDIENTS EXCEPT FISH SAUCE IN LARGE SAUCEPAN. BOIL GENTLY, COVERED, FOR ABOUT ONE HOUR.

REMOVE SCUM FROM SURFACE OCCASIONALLY AND DISCARD. REMOVE BONES AND STRAIN.

COOL UNCOVERED. REMOVE FAT FROM SURFACE OF STOCK.

ADD FISH SAUCE TO TASTE.

REFRIGERATE UNTIL NEEDED (CAN BE FROZEN) AND HEAT AGAIN WHEN PREPARING THE MEAL.

NEXT STEP:

500g/16oz FRESH, OR 200g/7oz DRIED, RICE NOODLES

QUICKLY BLANCH RICE NOODLES IN A LARGE SAUCEPAN OF BOILING WATER TO SOFTEN.

(FRESH NOODLES NEED WARMING ONLY, DON'T OVERCOOK.)

THEN YOU NEED TO HAVE READY:

200g/7oz RUMP STEAK, VERY FINELY SLICED (IT WILL BE EASIER IF YOU FREEZE IT FOR HALF AN HOUR FIRST)

1 SMALL ONION, VERY FINELY SLICED

2 SPRING ONIONS, FINELY SLICED

2 TABLESPOONS FRESH CORIANDER, CHOPPED

50-100g/1-2 CUPS BEAN SPROUTS

PUT NOODLES AND ONION INTO INDIVIDUAL SERVING BOWLS.

ARRANGE RUMP STEAK, SPRING ONIONS, CORIANDER AND BEAN SPROUTS IN BOWLS.

POUR HOT STOCK OVER TO JUST COVER, AND LEAVE FOR 2 MINUTES.

TOP UP WITH VERY HOT STOCK WHICH HAS BEEN BROUGHT BACK TO BOIL.

ADD MORE FISH SAUCE AND/OR CHILLI AS REQUIRED.

NOW GARNISH:

USE LIME WEDGES OR FRESH RED CHILLI, SLICED, OR ASIAN BASIL (RAU QUE), SHREDDED, OR LONG CORIANDER (NGO GAI), SHREDDED, OR BEAN SPROUTS, WASHED AND TRIMMED, OR VIETNAMESE MINT, OR MINT.

OR PUT THEM ALL ON THE TABLE IN SMALL BOWLS SO EVERYONE CAN HELP THEMSELVES.

CHILLI AND FISH SAUCE SHOULD ALSO BE AVAILABLE.

KEVIN BACON INVESTIGATING PHO BO
FROM UNDER THE SURFACE. HE WAS
EVENTUALLY ATTACKED BY A KNEEBONE AND IS
WRITING A FILM SCRIPT ABOUT THE INCIDENT

CA TIM NUONG

GRILLED EGGPLANT/AUBERGINE WITH STIR-FRIED PORK, LEMON AND GARLIC SAUCE
SERVES 4-6.

2 MEDIUM EGGPLANTS (AUBERGINES — CHOOSE THE LONG THIN ONES)

100g/4oz MINCED PORK

1 MEDIUM ONION, MINCED

1 CLOVE GARLIC

$1/2$ TEASPOON SALT

1 TEASPOON PEPPER

1 TABLESPOON OIL

1 TABLESPOON CHOPPED SPRING ONION

125ml/$1/2$ CUP LEMON AND GARLIC FISH SAUCE

MIX PORK WITH ONION, GARLIC, SALT AND $1/2$ THE PEPPER.

WASH AND DRY EGGPLANT/AUBERGINE.

PRICK EGGPLANTS WITH FORK, IF THE EGGPLANT/AUBERGINE IS MORE THAN 6 cm THICK, CUT IN HALF LENGTHWISE.

GRILL EGGPLANT/AUBERGINE AT MEDIUM HEAT. TURN OVER FREQUENTLY TO AVOID BURNING BEFORE THE VEGETABLE IS COOKED.

MEANWHILE, HEAT OIL IN FRYING PAN, ADD PORK MIXTURE. STIR-FRY UNTIL COOKED.

WHEN EGGPLANT/AUBERGINE IS TENDER AND SKIN IS LIGHTLY BURNT, REMOVE FROM HEAT.

SPRINKLE WITH REMAINDER OF PEPPER.

PLACE ON WARM PLATE AND SPREAD COOKED PORK ON TOP.

SPRINKLE WITH SPRING ONION AND REMAINING PEPPER.

POUR LEMON AND GARLIC FISH SAUCE ON TOP BEFORE SERVING.

SERVE WITH RICE.

DRAWING OF PINEAPPLE TO INCREASE
THE TROPICAL VERACITY OF THIS SMALL
BUT IMPORTANT BOOK

SATE GA BO

CHICKEN AND BEEF SATAYS

400g/14oz CHICKEN BREAST FILLETS
400g/14oz PIECE BEEF RUMP STEAK
125ml/$\frac{1}{2}$ CUP COCONUT MILK
60ml/$\frac{1}{4}$ CUP LIME JUICE
1 SMALL FRESH RED CHILLI, FINELY CHOPPED
3 SHALLOTS, FINELY CHOPPED
1 TABLESPOON FRESH BASIL, CHOPPED
3 CLOVES GARLIC, CRUSHED
1 TABLESPOON FISH SAUCE

SOAK BAMBOO SKEWERS IN WATER FOR SEVERAL HOURS OR OVERNIGHT TO PREVENT THEM FROM BURNING.

CUT CHICKEN AND BEEF INTO THIN STRIPS.

MARINATE WITH REMAINING INGREDIENTS IN BOWL. MIX WELL.

COVER MARINADE AND REFRIGERATE FOR SEVERAL HOURS.

DRAIN CHICKEN AND BEEF. DISCARD MARINADE.

THREAD CHICKEN AND BEEF SEPARATELY ONTO SKEWERS.

BARBECUE OR GRILL UNTIL BROWNED AND TENDER.

POUR EASY PEANUT SAUCE OVER.

SERVE WITH MINTED DIPPING SAUCE (ADD CHOPPED MINT TO NUOC MAM PAGE 22).

EASY PEANUT SAUCE:

60ml/¼ CUP HOI SIN SAUCE

60ml/¼ CUP CHICKEN STOCK

1 TABLESPOON FISH SAUCE

2 TABLESPOONS GROUND ROASTED UNSALTED PEANUTS

1 CHILLI, SEEDED AND SLICED

COMBINE HOI SIN, CHICKEN STOCK AND FISH SAUCE.

GARNISH WITH GROUND PEANUTS AND CHILLI.

FOR THIS ILLUSTRATION, PLEASE USE THE CAPTION ON PAGE 39, BUT SUBSTITUTE THE WORD 'PINEAPPLE' WITH THE WORDS 'TROPICAL RAINSTORM'.

(THE REUSE OF CAPTIONS BRINGS THIS BOOK TO YOU AT A REASONABLE PRICE)

DIA XA-LACH

TABLE SALAD

SERVES 6.

1 SOFT LETTUCE

100g/2 CUPS BEAN SPROUTS

3 CUCUMBERS, FINELY SLICED

3 LARGE SPRIGS OF MINT

2 SPRIGS OF HOT MINT

18 SMALL RICE-PAPER WRAPPERS (BANH TRANG)

1 QUANTITY CLASSIC DIPPING SAUCE

SEPARATE THE LETTUCE INTO LEAVES AND WASH AND DRY THEM. RINSE CLEAN AND TRIM BEAN SPROUTS. ARRANGE THE LETTUCE, VEGETABLES AND HERBS ON A LARGE PLATTER AND PUT THE RICE-PAPER WRAPPERS ON A SEPARATE PLATE.

TAKE A LARGE BOWL OF WARM WATER TO THE TABLE. DIP RICE PAPER IN WARM WATER FOR A FEW SECONDS TO SOFTEN. THE WRAPPER WILL SOFTEN IMMEDIATELY. (RICE-PAPER WRAPPERS SHOULDN'T BE SOAKED FOR MORE THAN A FEW SECONDS, AS THEY WILL BECOME TOO SOFT.)

TO EAT, PLACE THE LETTUCE, VEGETABLES, HERBS AND ANY DESIRED GRILLED MEAT OR SEAFOOD ON SOFTENED RICE PAPER AND ROLL.

SERVE WITH NUOC MAM CHAM NGUYEN CHAT AS THE DIPPING SAUCE (SEE PAGE 19).

GOI DU DU

GREEN PAPAYA SALAD

SERVES 4.

1 CHILLI, SEEDED, FINELY SLICED

2 CLOVES GARLIC, FINELY CHOPPED

1 TABLESPOON SUGAR

2 TABLESPOONS RICE VINEGAR

1 TABLESPOON FISH SAUCE

60ml/$\frac{1}{4}$ CUP WATER

1 PAPAYA (ABOUT 1kg/2 lb), PEELED, SEEDED AND SHREDDED OR GRATED

2 CARROTS, GRATED OR SHREDDED

2 TABLESPOONS CORIANDER, SHREDDED

8 LEAVES FRESH VIETNAMESE MINT

2 SLICES GRILLED DRIED BEEF, SHREDDED

COMBINE GARLIC, SUGAR, VINEGAR, CHILLI, FISH SAUCE AND WATER.

COMBINE PAPAYA AND CARROT.

PLACE ON SERVING PLATES.

TOP WITH BEEF, SHREDDED CORIANDER AND CHOPPED MINT.

GOI GA

CHICKEN SALAD

SERVES 6.

2 CHICKEN BREASTS
1/2 TEASPOON SALT
1/2 TEASPOON FRESHLY GROUND BLACK PEPPER
1 SMALL ONION, THINLY SLICED
2 TABLESPOONS SMALL AND TENDER HOT MINT (RAU RAM) LEAVES
1 TABLESPOON CRISP-FRIED SHALLOTS
1 FINELY-SHREDDED WHITE CABBAGE

DRESSING:

1 TEASPOON CHILLI SAUCE
1 CLOVE GARLIC, CRUSHED
125ml/1/2 CUP VINEGAR (OR TO TASTE)
4 TABLESPOONS LIME JUICE
1 TEASPOON FISH SAUCE
GROUND PEPPER

COMBINE ALL INGREDIENTS IN SCREW-TOP JAR, AND SHAKE.

PUT THE CHICKEN BREASTS IN A SAUCEPAN OF SALTED WATER AND BRING TO THE BOIL.

SIMMER UNTIL CHICKEN IS JUST COOKED THROUGH.
DRAIN AND COOL.

SHRED THE CHICKEN AND COMBINE IN A BOWL
WITH THE ONION AND HOT MINT.

STIR THE LIME JUICE DRESSING GENTLY THROUGH
THE CHICKEN AND SHREDDED CABBAGE.

TRANSFER THE SALAD TO A SERVING PLATTER AND
GARNISH WITH THE CRISP-FRIED SHALLOTS AND
LIME WEDGES.

EACH PERSON SQUEEZES LIME JUICE INTO A SMALL
SAUCE DISH AND MIXES IN A LITTLE SALT AND PEPPER
TO MAKE A DIPPING SAUCE.

IF DESIRED, PRAWN CRACKERS CAN BE USED TO
SCOOP UP THE SALAD.

UNNECESSARY PYRAMID

DAU PHU RIM

STIR-FRIED TOFU ON CRISP NOODLES

SERVES 4.

9 DRIED CHINESE MUSHROOMS

500g/1lb FIRM TOFU

60ml/$\frac{1}{4}$ CUP HOI SIN SAUCE

2 TABLESPOONS TOMATO SAUCE

2 TABLESPOONS FISH SAUCE

50g/$\frac{1}{4}$ CUP FINELY CHOPPED LEMON GRASS

2 SMALL FRESH RED CHILLIES, FINELY CHOPPED

1 LARGE ONION, FINELY CHOPPED

2 CLOVES GARLIC, CRUSHED

50g/$\frac{1}{4}$ CUP FRESH CORIANDER LEAVES, CHOPPED

100g/4oz THIN RICE STICK NOODLES

VEGETABLE OIL FOR FRYING

2 TEASPOONS PEANUT OIL

1 MEDIUM RED PEPPER, SLICED INTO THIN STRIPS (JULIENNE)

100g/4oz SNOW PEAS, SLICED INTO THIN STRIPS (JULIENNE)

COVER MUSHROOMS WITH BOILING WATER, LEAVE 20 MINUTES.

DRAIN, DISCARD STEMS AND SLICE CAPS INTO THIN STRIPS.

CUT TOFU INTO 3cm PIECES.

MIX GENTLY WITH SAUCES, LEMON GRASS, CHILLIES, ONION, GARLIC AND CORIANDER.

COVER AND STAND AT ROOM TEMPERATURE FOR 30 MINUTES.

DEEP-FRY NOODLES IN WOK IN HOT VEGETABLE OIL UNTIL PUFFED.

MARINATE TOFU IN LIQUID.

DRAIN ON ABSORBENT PAPER.

REMOVE TOFU FROM MARINADE (KEEP MARINADE).

HEAT PEANUT OIL AND LIGHTLY FRY TOFU UNTIL GOLDEN BROWN.

REMOVE FROM WOK.

ADD PEPPER, SNOW PEAS, MUSHROOMS AND RESERVED MARINADE TO WOK.

STIR-FRY FOR 3 MINUTES.

ADD TOFU AND HEAT THROUGH.

SERVE ON NOODLES.

BO XAO DAU ME

BEEF WITH SESAME SAUCE

SERVES 4.

250g/9oz RUMP STEAK

1 CLOVE GARLIC, CRUSHED

3 TABLESPOONS PEANUT OIL

125ml/$\frac{1}{2}$ CUP BEEF STOCK

1 TABLESPOON CORNFLOUR

2 TABLESPOONS COLD WATER

2 TEASPOONS SESAME PASTE (TAHINI)

$\frac{1}{2}$ TEASPOON CHILLI SAUCE

SLICE STEAK INTO STIR-FRY STRIPS.

HEAT PEANUT OIL IN A WOK, ADD GARLIC AND
MEAT AND STIR-FRY OVER HIGH HEAT UNTIL MEAT
HAS CHANGED COLOUR; ABOUT 2 MINUTES.

ADD STOCK AND BRING TO THE BOIL, THEN STIR IN
CORNFLOUR MIXED SMOOTHLY WITH COLD WATER.

STIR UNTIL IT BOILS AND THICKENS.

TURN OFF HEAT, STIR IN SESAME PASTE AND CHILLI
SAUCE. SERVE WITH WHITE RICE.

\# VARIATION: ADD MIXED VEGETABLES, CHINESE
   CABBAGE AND BAMBOO SHOOTS TO MAKE THIS
   A COMBINATION DISH.

SUON NUONG XA

MARINATED GRILLED PORK SPARE RIBS
WITH LEMON GRASS

SERVES 6.

- **2 SMALL CHILLIES**
- **4 SHALLOTS**
- **1 CLOVE GARLIC**
- **2 STALKS LEMON GRASS, FINELY CHOPPED**
- **1 TEASPOON SUGAR**
- **1 TABLESPOON FISH SAUCE**
- **1 TEASPOON SWEET SOY SAUCE**
- **1kg/2 lb PORK SPARE RIBS**

CRUSH THE GARLIC, SHALLOTS, CHILLIES AND
LEMON GRASS TOGETHER INTO A FINE PULP IN
A MORTAR.

ADD THE SUGAR.

STIR IN THE FISH SAUCE AND SOY SAUCE.

MARINATE THE SPARE RIBS IN A SHALLOW DISH
OVERNIGHT, OR FOR AT LEAST 3 HOURS, TURNING
OCCASIONALLY.

GRILL OR BARBECUE THE MARINATED SPARE RIBS.

COM CHAY

STIR-FRIED MIXED VEGETABLES

SERVES 4.

6 DRIED CHINESE MUSHROOMS
125ml/$^1/_2$ CUP WATER
1 TABLESPOON DARK SOY SAUCE
1 TEASPOON SESAME OIL
2 TEASPOONS SUGAR
3 STALKS CELERY
8 BABY BOK CHOY
$^1/_2$ SMALL LETTUCE
A FEW LEAVES OF MUSTARD CABBAGE
3 SPRING ONIONS
1 CLOVE GARLIC, FINELY CHOPPED
$^1/_2$ TEASPOON GRATED FRESH GINGER
1 TABLESPOON PEANUT OIL
1$^1/_2$ TABLESPOONS LIGHT SOY SAUCE
60ml/$^1/_4$ CUP WATER
1 TEASPOON CORNFLOUR
2 TABLESPOONS SHREDDED CORIANDER

SOAK DRIED MUSHROOMS IN HOT WATER FOR
30 MINUTES.

REMOVE AND DISCARD STEMS, SLICE TOPS THINLY, THEN SIMMER IN A SMALL SAUCEPAN WITH 125ml/$^1/_2$ CUP OF WATER, SOY SAUCE, SESAME OIL AND SUGAR UNTIL LIQUID IS ALMOST ABSORBED.

SLICE CELERY, BOK CHOY, MUSTARD CABBAGE AND LETTUCE INTO BITE-SIZE SQUARES AND SPRING ONION INTO SHORT LENGTHS.

FRY THE GARLIC AND GINGER IN PEANUT OIL OVER MEDIUM-LOW HEAT FOR A FEW SECONDS ONLY.

ADD LIGHT SOY SAUCE.

ADD STEMS OF VEGETABLES AND STIR-FRY OVER HIGH HEAT FOR 2 MINUTES.

ADD LEAFY PARTS AND FRY FOR 30 SECONDS.

ADD SAUCE AND PREPARED MUSHROOMS AND MIX TOGETHER.

ADD WATER, BRING TO THE BOIL.

THICKEN WITH CORNFLOUR BLENDED WITH A LITTLE COLD WATER.

STIR UNTIL IT BOILS AND THICKENS.

SERVE AT ONCE WITH RICE.

GARNISH WITH CORIANDER.

VIT QUAY

FENNEL-ROASTED DUCK WINGS

SERVES 4.

2 TABLESPOONS FISH SAUCE

4 CLOVES GARLIC, FINELY CHOPPED

250ml/1 CUP RED WINE VINEGAR

1 LARGE ONION, CHOPPED

2 TEASPOONS JUNIPER BERRIES, CRUSHED

2 TEASPOONS FENNEL SEEDS

4 DUCK WING PORTIONS

2 TABLESPOONS PLAIN YOGHURT

COMBINE FISH SAUCE, GARLIC, VINEGAR, ONION, BERRIES AND SEEDS IN BOWL.

PLACE DUCK IN SINGLE LAYER IN SHALLOW DISH, POUR OVER VINEGAR MIXTURE.

COVER DISH, REFRIGERATE FOR SEVERAL HOURS OR OVERNIGHT.

REMOVE DUCK FROM MARINADE (RESERVE MARINADE).

PLACE DUCK, SKIN SIDE UP, ON WIRE RACK OVER BAKING DISH.

BAKE, UNCOVERED, IN MODERATE OVEN FOR ABOUT 45 MINUTES OR UNTIL TENDER.

PLACE RESERVED MARINADE IN PAN, SIMMER, UNCOVERED, FOR ABOUT 5 MINUTES OR UNTIL SLIGHTLY THICKENED, THEN STRAIN.

STIR YOGHURT INTO SAUCE MIXTURE, SERVE WITH DUCK.

THIT HEO KHO TIEU

PORK STRIPS DRY-COOKED

SERVES 6-8.

750g/1 1/2 lb PORK NECK

2 TABLESPOONS WATER

2 TABLESPOONS FISH SAUCE

1 TABLESPOON SUGAR

3 SPRING ONIONS, THINLY SLICED

1/4 TEASPOON GROUND BLACK PEPPER

2 TABLESPOONS SHREDDED CORIANDER

CUT MEAT INTO THIN STRIPS. PUT INTO A SMALL, DEEP SAUCEPAN (A LARGE SAUCEPAN WILL NOT DO, AS THE LITTLE LIQUID THERE IS MUST SUFFICE FOR COOKING THE PORK AND NOT BE ALLOWED TO EVAPORATE FROM A LARGE SURFACE AREA).

ADD ALL OTHER INGREDIENTS EXCEPT CORIANDER AND BRING TO BOIL OVER HIGH HEAT, COVERED.

STIR, COOK FOR 2 MINUTES ON HIGH HEAT.

REDUCE HEAT TO MEDIUM AND BOIL FOR 20 MINUTES OR UNTIL LIQUID IS COMPLETELY ABSORBED.

STIR TOWARDS END OF COOKING SO THAT MEAT DOES NOT BURN.

PLACE ON SERVING DISH , SPRINKLE WITH SHREDDED CORIANDER.

SERVE WITH WHITE RICE AND GREEN VEGETABLES OR SALAD.

BO LUC LAC

SHAKING BEEF

SERVES 6.

300g/11 oz FILLET STEAK
1 CLOVE GARLIC, CRUSHED
1 TABLESPOON VEGETABLE OIL
2 TEASPOONS SUGAR

MARINADE:

1 CLOVE GARLIC, CRUSHED

1 TEASPOON SOY SAUCE

**1 TABLESPOON CHINESE RICE WINE
OR DRY SHERRY**

**GENEROUS PINCH OF FRESHLY
GROUND BLACK PEPPER**

1 TEASPOON SUGAR

MIX THE MARINADE INGREDIENTS IN A DEEP DISH.

CUT THE FILLET INTO 2cm CUBES AND MARINATE FOR AN HOUR OR TWO, TURNING FROM TIME TO TIME.

HEAT THE OIL IN A WOK WITH THE GARLIC.

WHEN THE OIL IS HOT, ADD THE BEEF CUBES AND SHAKE THE PAN VIGOROUSLY TO MAKE SURE THAT THEY ARE ALL WELL SEARED ON ALL SIDES BUT STILL RARE INSIDE.

SPRINKLE SUGAR OVER THE MEAT AND KEEP
SHAKING THE WOK SO THAT THE SUGAR MELTS
AND COMBINES WITH THE PAN JUICES TO
CARAMELISE AND GLAZE THE BEEF CUBES.

SERVE IMMEDIATELY.

CAN BE SERVED WITH SLICED CUCUMBER OR
A MIXED SALAD, OR JUST WITH RICE.

THANK YOU FOR NOT ASKING
WHY THIS PARTICULAR ILLUSTRATION
HAS BEEN USED

CA NUONG THAN

BARBECUED WHOLE FISH

SERVES 6.

**1 WHOLE SNAPPER OR BREAM,
CLEANED AND GUTTED
(APPROXIMATELY 1kg/2 lb)**

3 TEASPOONS SALT

**1 TEASPOON FRESHLY GROUND
BLACK PEPPER**

1 LIME, SLICED

3 TABLESPOONS VEGETABLE OIL

1 MEDIUM ONION, SLICED

1 CLOVE GARLIC, SLICED

GARNISH:

**1 TABLESPOON GINGER, FRESHLY
SHREDDED**

3 SPRING ONIONS, FINELY SHREDDED

**2 TABLESPOONS SHREDDED
CORIANDER**

WASH THE FISH AND DRY IT WELL.

RUB IT ALL OVER WITH THE SALT AND PEPPER AND
PUT THE LIME SLICES IN ITS STOMACH CAVITY.

ALLOW THE FISH TO STAND FOR ABOUT 30 MINUTES.

CUT 2 OR 3 DIAGONAL SLASHES INTO EACH SIDE OF THE FISH TO ALLOW FOR FAST, EVEN COOKING.

PUT THE FISH ON THE GRILL AND COOK UNTIL THE FLESH IS COOKED THROUGH BUT STILL FIRM.

WHEN THE FISH IS ALMOST READY, HEAT THE OIL AND FRY THE ONION AND GARLIC UNTIL GOLDEN BROWN.

PUT THE COOKED FISH ON A SERVING PLATE AND POUR THE HOT OIL AND ONION MIXTURE OVER IT.

GARNISH WITH GINGER, SPRING ONION AND CORIANDER AND SERVE IMMEDIATELY.

THIS FISH CAN BE SERVED WITH RICE VERMICELLI OR RICE AND A TABLE SALAD OF LETTUCE, BEAN SPROUTS, MINTS (HOT OR ORDINARY) AND LONG CORIANDER.

CHE CHUOI

BANANAS IN COCONUT MILK

SERVES 6.

3 TABLESPOONS SUGAR

GENEROUS PINCH OF SALT

1 TEASPOON LIME JUICE

500ml/2 CUPS COCONUT MILK

3 RIPE BUT FIRM BANANAS, PEELED (NOT SUGAR BANANAS, THEY WILL BECOME BITTER)

DISSOLVE SUGAR WITH SALT AND LIME JUICE IN SAUCEPAN OVER LOW HEAT.

ADD COCONUT MILK AND BRING TO BOIL, UNCOVERED.

SLICE BANANAS LENGTHWISE AND THEN ACROSS INTO 4 PIECES.

ADD TO SIMMERING COCONUT MILK MIXTURE AND COOK GENTLY FOR A FEW MINUTES (YOU WANT THEM SOFT BUT NOT MUSHY).

SERVE WARM.

KEM VAI

LYCHEE AND GINGER ICE

SERVES 4.

1 565g/18oz CAN LYCHEES
1 TABLESPOON FINELY GRATED FRESH GINGER (OR PRESERVED)
125ml/$^1/_2$ CUP LIME JUICE
85ml/$^1/_3$ CUP WATER (APPROXIMATELY)
150g/$^3/_4$ CUP CASTOR SUGAR
1 EGG WHITE

DRAIN LYCHEES AND SAVE LIQUID.

BLEND OR PROCESS LYCHEES AND GINGER UNTIL COMBINED. COMBINE RESERVED LIQUID AND LIME JUICE.

ADD ENOUGH WATER TO MAKE 500ml/2 CUPS.

COMBINE LYCHEE MIXTURE WITH LIQUID AND SUGAR IN SAUCEPAN AND STIR OVER HEAT UNTIL SUGAR IS MELTED.

DON'T BOIL.

COOL, POUR MIXTURE INTO A 20 X 30 cm SHALLOW PAN.

COVER AND FREEZE UNTIL JUST FIRM.

BREAK UP MIXTURE WITH A FORK. PUT IN BLENDER OR PROCESSOR WITH EGG WHITE UNTIL SMOOTH.

RETURN TO PAN, COVER, AND FREEZE UNTIL FIRM.

BANH CHUOI
VIETNAMESE BANANA CAKE

600g/1 1/4 lb RIPE BANANAS

8-10 SLICES TOAST BREAD, CRUSTS REMOVED

2 TABLESPOONS SUGAR

250ml/1 CUP COCONUT CREAM

STIR SUGAR INTO COCONUT CREAM.

SOAK BREAD IN SUGAR/COCONUT CREAM MIXTURE.

MASH BANANAS AND MOISTENED BREAD TOGETHER WELL.

POUR INTO GREASED LOAF TIN.

BAKE UNCOVERED AT 180°C/350°F/GAS MARK 4 FOR 1 HOUR OR UNTIL GOLDEN.

REMOVE FROM OVEN AND STAND FOR 10 MINUTES BEFORE REMOVING FROM TIN.

THERE ARE NO
UNDERPANT JOKES
IN THIS BOOK

TWELVE THINGS YOU NEED TO KNOW TO PRETEND YOU'RE AN EXPERT VIETNAMESE COOK.

1 CHINA OCCUPIED VIETNAM FOR 10 CENTURIES. THIS INFLUENCED THE FOOD.

2 FRANCE OCCUPIED VIETNAM FROM 1859-1954. THIS INFLUENCED THE FOOD.

3 LAOS AND CAMBODIA SHARE BORDERS WITH VIETNAM. THIS INFLUENCED THE FOOD.

4 THE UNITED STATES OF AMERICA TOOK OVER VIETNAM IN THE '60S AND '70S. THIS DIDN'T INFLUENCE THE FOOD AT ALL.

5 YOU MUST NOT ATTEMPT TO COOK VIETNAMESE WITHOUT FIRST ESTABLISHING A SUPPLY OF FISH SAUCE, PREFERABLY VIETNAMESE-STYLE. YOU MAY FIND SOME AT YOUR DELI, IF YOU'RE LUCKY, OR YOU MAY NEED TO FIND YOURSELF AN ASIAN SUPERMARKET (YOU WILL NEED ONE FOR SOME OF THE OTHER INGREDIENTS). IT IS USED IN VIETNAM LIKE SALT. MIX IT WITH GARLIC, CHILLI, SUGAR AND LIME OR LEMON JUICE AND IT BECOMES A NUOC MAM DIPPING SAUCE.

6 YOU CAN ADD NUOC MAM TO PRACTICALLY EVERYTHING (AS A SAUCE OR AS A DIPPING SAUCE).

7 BREAKFAST IN VIETNAM IS USUALLY NOODLE SOUP OR RICE WITH PICKLES.

8 MAIN MEALS ARE RICE WITH 3 OR 4 DISHES, AND EVERYONE EATS FROM A SMALL INDIVIDUAL DISH WITH CHOPSTICKS. SOUP IS ADDED IN ORDER TO MOISTEN THE MEAL.

9 SMALL BOWLS OF A VARIETY OF DIPPING SAUCES AT THE TABLE ARE AN INTEGRAL PART OF YOUR AVERAGE VIETNAMESE MEAL AND ADD A WEALTH OF FLAVOUR TO THE MOST MODEST FOOD.

10 VEGETABLES, SEAFOOD, PORK AND CHICKEN ARE THE MOST FREQUENTLY EATEN INGREDIENTS, WITH RICE OR RICE NOODLES SERVED WITH EVERYTHING.

11 ACCOMPANIMENTS ARE CRUCIAL, AND EASY. THE PLAINEST MEAL IN VIETNAM WILL BE SERVED WITH A VARIETY OF ADDITIONAL BITS AND PIECES (AS WELL AS DIPPING SAUCES).

12 NO-ONE IN AMERICA KNOWS THAT TOM CRUISE IS NOT LIVING AMONG THEM.

SOME OF THE INGREDIENTS YOU MIGHT NOT HAVE HEARD OF YET

RAU QUE ASIAN BASIL

PURPLE STEMS, ANISEED SCENT. ADD TO SOUPS, TABLE SALADS.

DAU HU AKA TOFU BEANCURD

BOILED, CRUSHED SOY BEANS, COAGULATED TO FORM A BLOCK.

BUY FRESH FIRM TOFU AND KEEP IT REFRIGERATED.

CAY CUC CHRYSANTHEMUM GREENS

SOLD IN BUNCHES IN ASIAN FOOD STORES.

EAT RAW IN SOUPS OR SALADS.

DUA COCONUT CREAM

BUY IN SUPERMARKET.

BUY COCONUT MILK (NOT THE LIQUID INSIDE COCONUT) FROM SUPERMARKET ALSO.

NGO CORIANDER

LEAVES USED AS GARNISH – AVAILABLE AT MOST GREENGROCERS.

GUNG GINGER

FLAVOUR FOR SOUPS, MARINADES, MAIN DISHES.

GRATE, CHOP OR SLICE.

NUOC MAM FISH SAUCE

CLEAR SAUCE MADE FROM ANCHOVIES FERMENTED IN SALT.

ADD TO MARINADES, MAIN COURSES AND DIPPING SAUCES.

IN VIETNAM IT'S USED IN PLACE OF SALT.

NUOC MAM LENDS ITS NAME TO THE DIPPING SAUCE OF THE SAME NAME (PAGE 22).

HOI SIN SAUCE

THICK AND SWEET, MADE FROM SALTED BLACK BEANS, ONIONS AND GARLIC.

XA LEMON GRASS

GRASS-LIKE HERB, AVAILABLE FRESH FROM ASIAN FOOD STORES, AND EASY TO GROW.

ESSENTIAL INGREDIENT IN SOUPS, MARINADES, STIR-FRIES, CURRIES.

RAU RAM VIETNAMESE MINT (HOT MINT)

HAS LONG PURPLISH LEAVES AND A PUNGENT FLAVOUR.

ADDED TO STRONGLY FLAVOURED DISHES.

ALSO USED IN TABLE SALADS.

HOI STAR ANISE

LIQUORICE/ANISEED-FLAVOURED HERB.
ESSENTIAL INGREDIENT IN PHO SOUP.

CU CAI TRAN WHITE RADISH

USED IN SALADS AND PICKLES. OR GRATED RAW INTO DIPPING SAUCES.